EXECUTIVE FUNCTIONING

Workbook for Kids

A Fun Adventure with Bora the Space Cat
to Learn How to Plan, Prioritize, and
Set Goals in Everyday Life

ROY D. PAN, PH.D., EDCHIEVE, LLC

Illustrations by Valentina Plazas

Paperback ISBN: 979-8-9863493-0-5

Table of Contents

Special Offer

Sign up to get a free crystal and treasure chest printout your child can use on this journey. You'll also get free resources as they become available!

Visit www.edchievellc.com/publishing

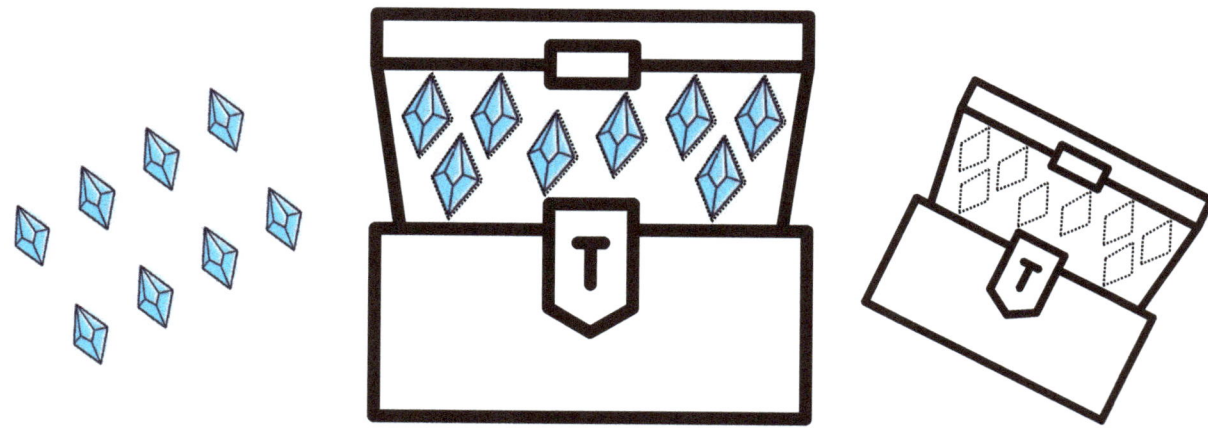

Note to Grown-Ups

Welcome! We are about to embark on a mission to work on your child's executive functioning skills so that they can be successful in school, future careers, and everyday life. This book is the first of my executive functions series that will cover all of the executive functioning skills in-depth. We will focus on **planning, prioritizing, and setting goals** in this book. Other skills will be covered in subsequent books.

My name is Roy Pan. I am a UCLA Ph.D. and a seasoned education professional. I have helped hundreds of students achieve both academic and personal success throughout my career.

I started Edchieve, LLC to help students tackle executive functioning challenges. Through my work, I have learned that many families face similar issues. After countless hours of teaching the same skills and seeing great results, I decided to publish this book to share my methods with many other families in need.

This book is designed to help young children tackle executive functioning challenges before they manifest into bigger issues in the future. The activities and the underlying education principles in this workbook have been thoroughly tested by education professionals. Although this book is generally designed for ages 9 to 12, older or younger children may still find it helpful depending on their individual progress and development.

As children become teenagers, they get more reluctant to work on the skills that give them trouble. By this time, they likely have had many adults reprimand them for their shortcomings. They are often told that they are lazy, not trying hard enough, or do not care. Over time, they typically shut down after repeatedly hearing this type of negative talk. In some instances, they start losing confidence and may internalize negative feelings about their academic performances and behaviors, leading to even less motivation to improve.

Early intervention is key to preventing this type of vicious cycle. It is typically easier to instill good habits early before bad habits settle in. As adults, we have to proactively try to identify their challenges since they often do not ask for help. They simply do not know what they do not know. In many instances, these problems are caused by executive functioning deficits.

This book is designed to help children address these issues before they manifest into bigger problems. It is meant to be somewhat challenging, so it is normal for children to feel frustrated and lose interest from time to time. As adults, our role is to encourage them to learn independently yet provide timely support when they feel challenged. One useful way to help them when they feel like giving up is to ask them why instead of jumping to conclusions. That way, we will be able to help them address the challenges more accurately. This will also help them feel more heard and understood.

As your child finishes each chapter, please go over the answers and discuss key points to ensure they truly understand the material. By doing so regularly, you will be able to redirect your child before they stray too far. Inevitably, your child will make mistakes. When offering criticism, try making a compliment sandwich. Point out what was done well, introduce the criticism next, then provide another compliment to finish. This proven technique will help anyone digest feedback more favorably, and it will also help children stay motivated.

A unique component of this book is that the lessons are embedded into a space adventure with the promise of a reward at the end. Readers will visit eight planets as they work through the book, each awarding them one fictional prize, the crystal, upon completion. Once they have collected all eight crystals, they are promised a final reward for completing the mission.

The final reward is extremely important because human actions are significantly driven by the reward system. Providing a reward creates excitement to learn and improves confidence when it is obtained. Please agree on a reward with your child before they embark on this journey. Feel free to choose whatever you are comfortable with providing, but make sure it is something special that your child will get excited to work for—making this journey more fun for all parties involved!

If you are reading this book, I am sure you can understand how important it is for children to hone their executive functioning skills early and often. This book has all the right tools to help children open the doors to success.

Get started right now and see your child conquer massive challenges for years to come!

Note to Kids

Bora, the Space Cat:

"Welcome, hero! Thank you for joining us on this very important mission to save the world! Planet Earth is currently under attack by scary aliens. We have chosen you as our brave hero to help us gather eight valuable crystals to unlock the Stargate portal and send the aliens away. So get on your spaceship and visit different planets to complete the challenges! You will get a crystal after conquering each planet. After you collect all eight crystals and save Planet Earth, you will get a reward in real life for your bravery! Good luck—humanity is counting on you!"

The reward is something you agree on with your trusted adult. Please write down the reward below and make sure your trusted adult agrees to it by giving their signature.

Reward: _____

Signature: _____

Signature: _____

Quick Note Before Getting Started:

The challenges in this workbook can help you master executive functioning skills wherever you are. After completing this workbook, you will gain the confidence and skill set to conquer many difficult real-life problems. As you read through the chapters and complete the challenges at your own pace, you will begin to see your skills develop. You will slowly notice that you are better at completing your daily tasks and achieving your personal goals. The activities in this workbook will inspire you to learn more about executive functioning skills and confirm the exceptional talents you have always possessed. Good luck on your journey!

As you complete the challenges in this workbook, try to share what you learned with your friends and family within a day or two. This is the best way to help you master the material!

"As you can see, the aliens have already invaded Planet Earth. We need your help to open the secret portal, Stargate. Each planet hosts one crystal each— with the first one being on Planet Earth. Collect all eight crystals, and you will get the reward promised to you at the beginning! Are you ready? Let's begin!"

Welcome on Board!

Collect 8 crystals
to open Stargate

Challenge 1

Design Your Character

Start the journey in style! In the box below, draw yourself as the hero going on this mission. Also, write down three of your strengths and draw items around your character to represent them—these are the superpowers you can rely on when times get rough!

Hero Name: ____________________

Your Strengths:

1. ____________________
2. ____________________
3. ____________________

Bora, the Space Cat:

"Good job completing this first step, and congratulations on getting the first crystal! Let's head out to the next planet to learn what executive functioning skills are and collect the next crystal."

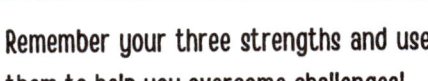

Remember your three strengths and use them to help you overcome challenges!

Planet Priority

Planet Goals

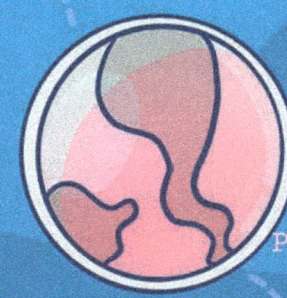
Planet Planner

Planet Knowledge

Planet Skills

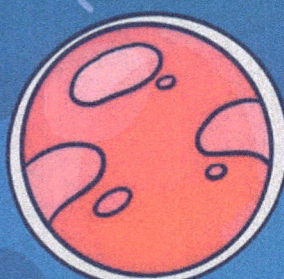
Planet Reflection

Next
Stop

Planet Executive

You Are
Here →

Planet Earth

10

Chapter 2
Planet Executive

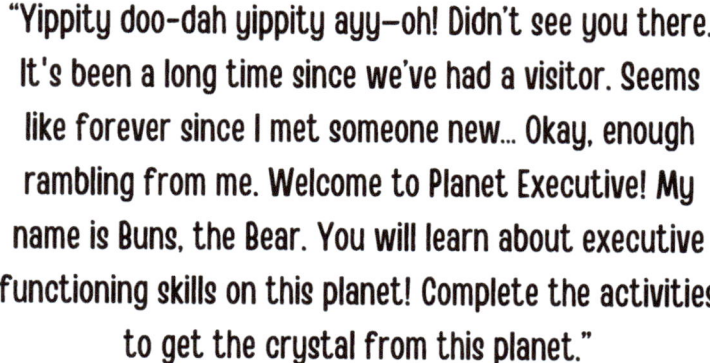

"Yippity doo-dah yippity ayy—oh! Didn't see you there. It's been a long time since we've had a visitor. Seems like forever since I met someone new... Okay, enough rambling from me. Welcome to Planet Executive! My name is Buns, the Bear. You will learn about executive functioning skills on this planet! Complete the activities to get the crystal from this planet."

What are Executive Functioning Skills?

Have you ever wondered how singers prepare for concerts or how detectives solve mysteries? They use executive functioning skills!

Executive functioning skills are the skills that assist us in concentrating, completing tasks, remembering important things, and organizing things in our brain. They help us think about how to do tasks and get started on them, where we should put things and find them, and when events and important celebrations are supposed to happen. Executive functioning skills are important to develop because as you get older, you will need to keep track of your schedule and complete tasks on time—all by yourself! Learning how to identify what you need to do and how to get it done efficiently are ways to develop executive functioning skills. If you want to be better at organizing your room, focusing on one task at a time, or handing in homework on time, then learning the skills in this workbook will help you tremendously.

All About Executive Functioning Skills

Read the following sentences and decide whether it is true or false by circling one of the two options. Try your best and ask for help if you are stuck.

1. I can use executive functioning skills to overcome difficult challenges.

True   **False**

2. Adults do not use executive functioning skills.

True   **False**

3. Executive functioning skills are only used in school.

True   **False**

4. I need executive functioning skills to play sports.

True   **False**

5. Executive functioning skills can help me plan fun trips with my family.

True   **False**

6. I don't need executive functioning skills to do everyday tasks.

True   **False**

7. Learning new executive functioning skills is possible.

True   **False**

8. I can improve my executive functioning skills by practicing every day.

True   **False**

9. Only executives use executive functioning skills.

True   **False**

10. I use executive functioning skills to learn, read, and do homework.

True   **False**

Getting to Know Me

"I'll give you the crystal you need if you can complete the exercise below. Feel free to write down anything that comes to mind and refer to the previous pages if you are stuck. There are no wrong answers!"

Complete the following sentences by circling the bolded words in the boxes. Choose all that apply to you. Feel free to add anything else you can think of on the dotted lines.

1 Learning executive functioning skills will help me...

concentrate	**prioritize**	**plan**	**set goals**
learn	**organize**	**be on time**	

....

2 I can accomplish these things with executive functioning skills...

ride a bike	**organize my room**	**my dream goal**
plan fun trips	**cook a meal**	**sing at a concert**

....

Buns, the Bear:

"Wow, those are great reasons! You inspire me to learn more about executive functioning skills. Well, here is the crystal you are looking for."

You just received another crystal. You now have two and need six more to go!

Planning and prioritizing are two of the most important executive functioning skills. Head over to the next planet to learn more about them and collect the next crystal.

Break Time: Spend 10 minutes teaching someone what you just learned. Sharing what you learned will help you understand better!

Planet Priority

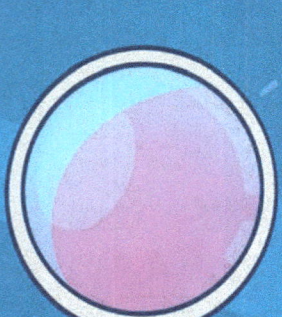

Planet Goals

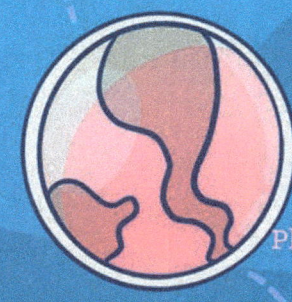

Planet Planner

Planet Knowledge

Next Stop

Planet Skills

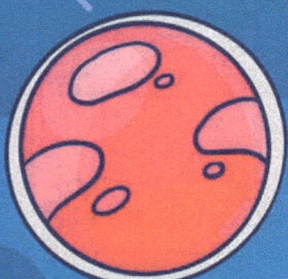

Planet Reflection

You Are Here

Planet Executive

Planet Earth

Chapter 3
Planet Skills

"Welcome to Planet Skills! My name is Scooter. You will learn about planning and prioritizing on this planet. By the way, we dinosaurs are not as scary as people on Earth say. We're tired of people not wanting to be our friends because they assume we are mean. I mean, have they not seen Rex from Toy Story? Anyway... are you ready for the next challenge? Here we go!"

How to Plan and Prioritize

Do you find it difficult to complete various unexciting tasks every day? Most of us have to go to school, do chores, complete homework, bathe, eat, clean up, and brush our teeth every day—and that is just a short list! As you grow older, your list will grow longer and longer. Everyone gets frustrated when their day ends before they can get everything done. The key to avoiding these frustrations is to know how to plan and prioritize different tasks.

Story Time 📅

Scooter, the Dinosaur, is a busy dinosaur with many things to do each day. At first, he just did whatever he felt like doing, and sometimes he even started multiple tasks at once. He frequently struggled with planning and prioritizing. After a while, he realized that his system needed to be improved. He was not completing his tasks even though he was often exhausted at the end of the day. Eventually, he decided to work on his planning and prioritizing skills to help him become more effective. After working on his planning and prioritizing skills every day, he now has a whole calendar system that allows him to easily plan out his daily tasks and complete them in the best order possible without feeling stressed. His progress is paying off every day.

So What Exactly Is Planning and Prioritizing?

Planning

- Think about what you need to do and save time to do them.
- Save plenty of time for each task.
- Be prepared for things to take longer than you think.
- Practice makes perfect!

There are several ways to get better at planning, which we will learn in the next chapter!

Pro Tip: Improving your planning skills will help you figure out how much time you need for each task so you can complete them on time! ⏰

Prioritizing

- Think about what needs to be done first before starting your to-do list.
- Decide the order you should complete each task.
- Start with the most important tasks first instead of the easiest ones.
- Prioritizing helps you become more efficient!

Sometimes, it is not easy to see which task needs to be completed first. We will go over useful strategies in Chapter 5.

Pro Tip: Improving your prioritizing skills will help you complete the important tasks first, so you don't lose track of time! ⏰

More and more aliens are arriving on Planet Earth. We need a brave hero to help us!

Color Me

In other news, all anyone is talking about on social media is the brave hero! The spaceship blasting off is getting lots of views!

Questionnaire

Let's get to know you a little better! Read the following sentences and circle the choice that most accurately describes your actions. There is no right or wrong answer here. Just try to answer as best as you can.

1. My homework or classwork is either late or not turned in at all.

   Never   **Sometimes**   **Often**   **Always**

2. When I have to do a big project, I do most of the work on the last day.

   Never   **Sometimes**   **Often**   **Always**

3. I usually need more time for my assignments than I previously thought.

   Never   **Sometimes**   **Often**   **Always**

4. I have trouble finishing my chores.

   Never   **Sometimes**   **Often**   **Always**

5. I find it hard to choose a goal.

   Never   **Sometimes**   **Often**   **Always**

6. I forget to bring homework or important things to school.

   Never   **Sometimes**   **Often**   **Always**

7. My teacher tells me I am missing parts of my homework.

   Never   **Sometimes**   **Often**   **Always**

8. I usually take a long time to get ready.

   Never   **Sometimes**   **Often**   **Always**

9. I need lots of reminders to stay on track with my tasks.

   Never   **Sometimes**   **Often**   **Always**

10. When I have a lot of tasks to do, I am not sure where to start.

   Never   **Sometimes**   **Often**   **Always**

11. I forget what I have to do next and need reminders.

Never   **Sometimes**   **Often**   **Always**

12. I have trouble finding things in my room.

Never   **Sometimes**   **Often**   **Always**

13. I have big dreams, but I don't know how to achieve them.

Never   **Sometimes**   **Often**   **Always**

14. I get frustrated when I need to plan.

Never   **Sometimes**   **Often**   **Always**

Never	Sometimes	Often	Always

Take a moment to count how many you circled for each one and write the total number in the box above. If you circled mostly "always," that means you should benefit by practicing the skills in this book. If you circled mostly "never," you might already have some good habits and only need to learn some useful tricks. Everyone has their strengths and weaknesses—even Superman is scared of kryptonite! If you find that you lack certain skills, you can always learn and get better by practicing every day.

Fill in the Blank

"I'll give you the crystal you need if you can complete these sentences!"

Read the following questions and fill in the blanks with one of the two words. Choose the word that fits best with each sentence, and refer to pages 18 and 20 if you get stuck.

| Planning | or | Prioritizing |

1 .... involves thinking about what you need to do and saving time to do them.

| Planning | or | Prioritizing |

2 .... involves asking the question: are there any tasks I need to complete before others?

| watch | or | calendar |

3 Scooter, the Dinosaur, uses a .... to help him to help him plan his daily tasks.

| challenging | or | easier |

4 It often makes more sense to complete the .... tasks first.

| time | or | space |

5 Taking a few minutes to think about which tasks to do first before working on them may save me lots of ....

Scooter, the Dinosaur:

"Amazing! You are on the right track to becoming an expert in planning and prioritizing! Effective planning and prioritizing will make you feel more accomplished, efficient, and happy. That reminds me... I need to work on my skills, too. Here is the crystal you are looking for! I hope you enjoyed this planet. Please give us a five-star rating! Haha, just kidding."

You just received another crystal. You now have three and need five more to complete the set!

Planning involves creating routines, schedules, and checklists. All those tasks require deciding which smaller steps to prioritize first. We will go over different ways to plan and prioritize in the following two chapters. Now, let's head to the next planet for your fourth crystal.

Break Time: Spend 10 minutes teaching someone what you just learned. Sharing what you learned will help you understand better!

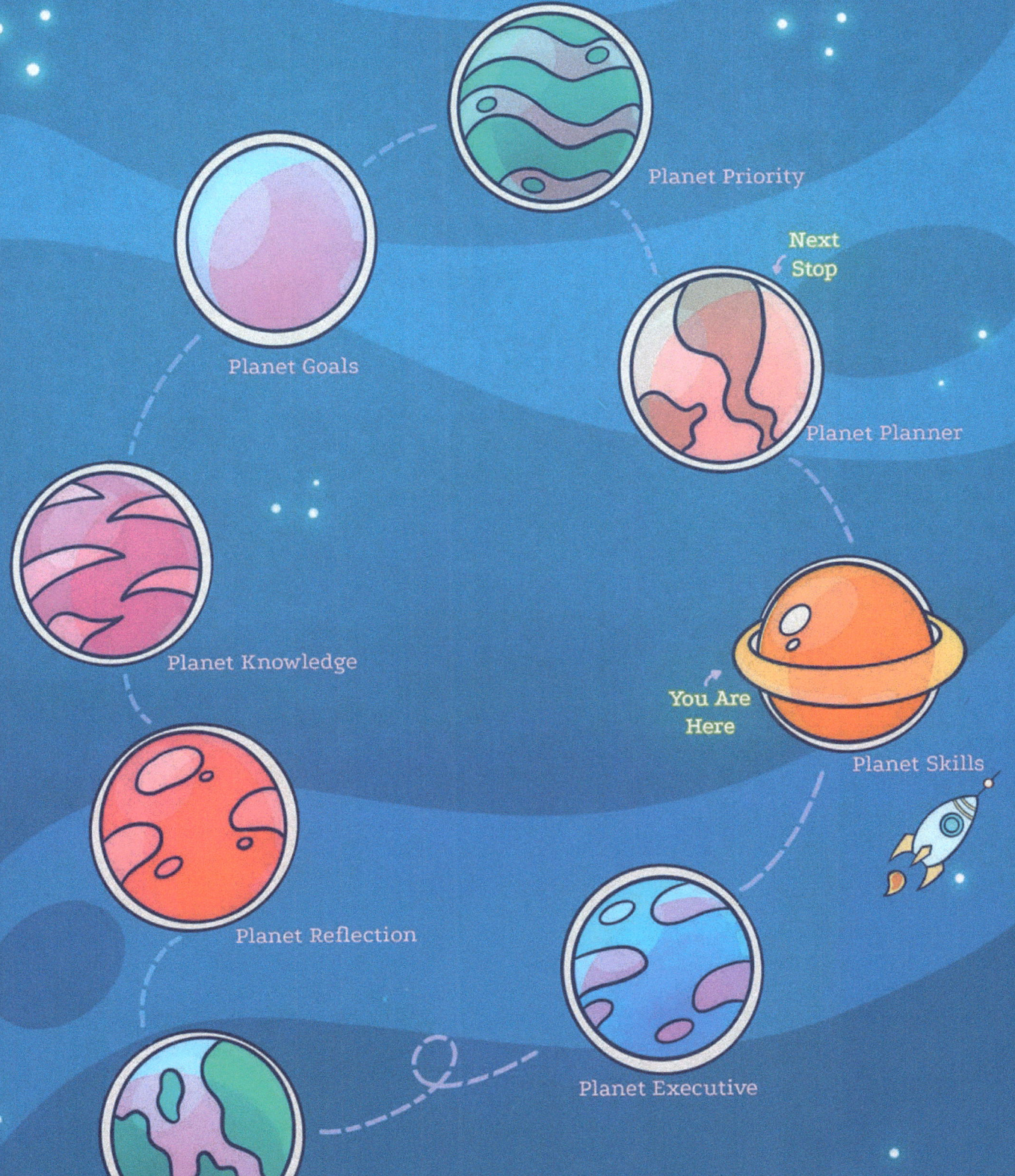

Planet Priority

Next Stop

Planet Goals

Planet Planner

Planet Knowledge

You Are Here

Planet Skills

Planet Reflection

Planet Executive

Planet Earth

Chapter 4
Planet Planner

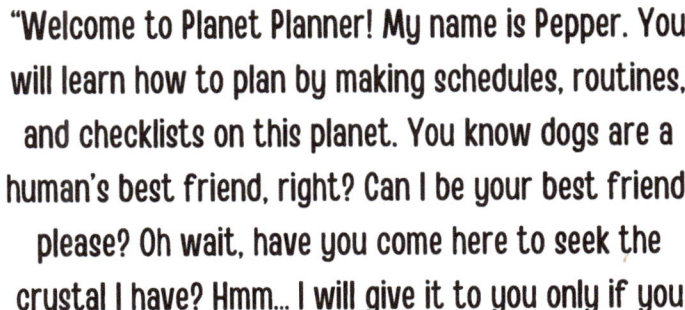

"Welcome to Planet Planner! My name is Pepper. You will learn how to plan by making schedules, routines, and checklists on this planet. You know dogs are a human's best friend, right? Can I be your best friend, please? Oh wait, have you come here to seek the crystal I have? Hmm... I will give it to you only if you complete the challenges here!"

Planning Skills Deep Dive

Planning is the ability to think ahead. It is what makes us humans more intelligent than most animals. It requires one to look into the future and predict what needs to be done to achieve a goal—like how Dr. Strange saw the future and helped the Avengers win Infinity War! Without detailed planning, things usually do not turn out well because human beings are forgetful creatures. For instance, if you forget to bring your permission slip to school, you might miss out on a fun field trip with your classmates.

Did you know?

- Successful people always plan before doing important tasks.
- Experienced planners can predict the future using their past experiences.
- For example, your teachers may prepare extra worksheets because they have seen people lose them before. They will not need to leave class for more copies if they prepare extra.
- Knowing how to plan will help you save lots of time!

Color Me

Why Is Planning Important?

Planning is very important for young students like you, especially in school. Students who plan well usually get better grades, study less, and enjoy school more. It is also important outside of school. Events like parties, games, and fun trips require good planning to go smoothly. Everything is always easier and much more successful when properly planned.

You might think: I want to plan ahead and enjoy success, but how do I get better at planning? Planning a task can seem intimidating at first, but there are many helpful ways to do it. That is what you will learn in this chapter. Work through the challenges in this chapter, and you shall have a much better grasp of the necessary planning skills. After learning these skills, you will get in the habit of planning, and you will realize that difficult tasks often get easier with proper planning. These strategies should continue to help as you grow up and take on more challenging tasks.

Remember your three strengths and use them to help you overcome challenges!

Break Down Hard Tasks

Have you ever had to do something that seemed so difficult you were unsure where to start? The exercise below should help!

Start by scoring the difficult task on a scale of 1-10: 1 being super easy and 10 being almost impossible. Tasks that score greater than 4 should be broken down into easier steps. Your goal is to break down difficult tasks into easier, level 3 steps.

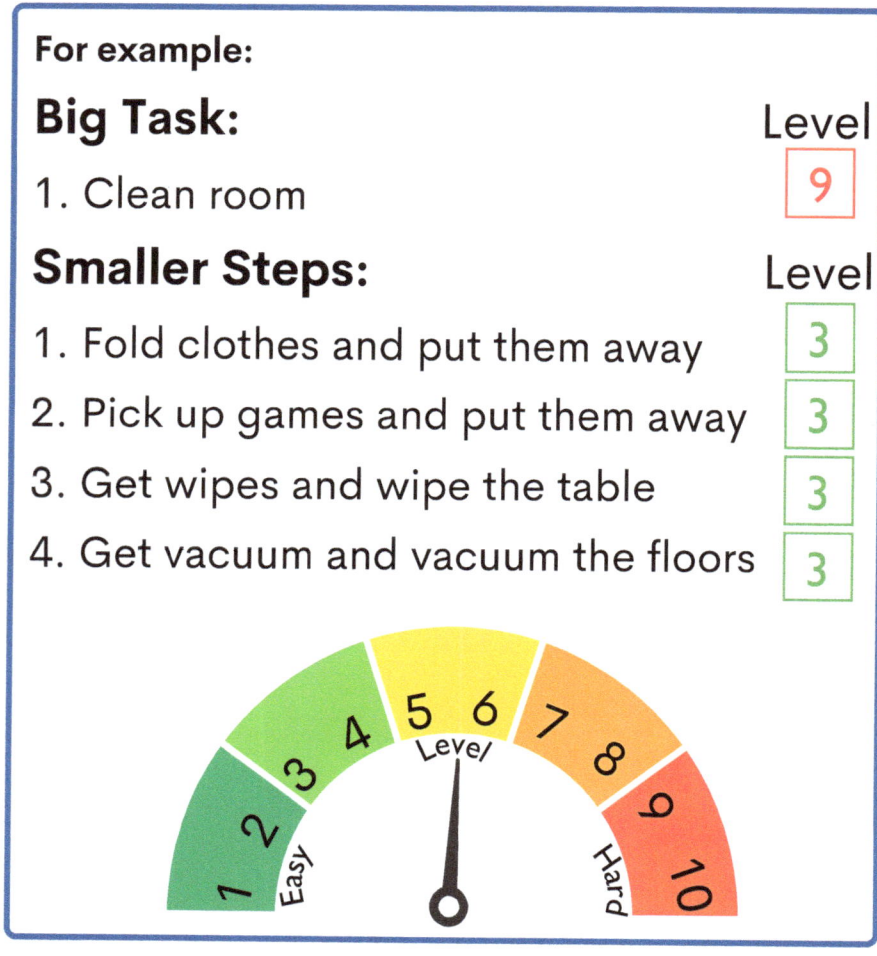

For example:

Big Task: Level
1. Clean room   9

Smaller Steps: Level
1. Fold clothes and put them away   3
2. Pick up games and put them away   3
3. Get wipes and wipe the table   3
4. Get vacuum and vacuum the floors   3

In the above example, the difficult task of cleaning your room is broken down into smaller and more defined steps. This will assist you in creating a clear plan for completing the task. Use this as an example only. Each task's difficulty level may be different for each person, and there is no right or wrong answer. It is also okay to take short breaks between each small step if you really need one. A short break would be a 5-10 min break. Any longer breaks would not be a short break and may make it harder to get back on track.

It is your turn to try this strategy! Write down one hard task that is a level 8 or above. Break up the task into easier level 3 steps. Make sure to talk to your trusted adult if you need some ideas.

Big Task: **Level**

1. _____

Smaller Steps: **Level**

1. _____

2. _____

3. _____

4. _____

Now, the difficult task suddenly looks more doable, right?

Homework Planning

Let's look at how Pepper, the Dog, does his homework planning after he comes home from school.

1. Check which materials are required.
2. Rate each homework by the level of difficulty.
3. Decide which one will take longer to complete and require more effort.
4. Break down the most challenging one into smaller steps and tackle each step one by one.
5. Start homework early and ask for help if needed.

He realizes that breaking down the difficult assignment into smaller steps makes it easier to complete because he can see exactly how he will finish it.

Like Pepper, you can practice homework planning by answering the questions below. If you do not have any homework, you can save this section and return to it later.

1. When are my homework assignments due?

_____

2. How many days do I have until the deadlines?

_____

3. What materials do I need?

_____

4. Do I understand the instructions? If not, who can I ask for help?

_____

5. Which homework do I think is the most difficult?

_____

6. How can I break up the most difficult homework into smaller tasks?

_____

_____

_____

You can always check your progress with a trusted adult and ask for help if needed. There is always room for improvement. With practice, you will get better at planning!

Daily Routines and Checklists

Do you often experience chaotic mornings when you rush to school and forget important items like books or homework? Creating a daily routine that you do every day can help. For example, a great way to have an easy morning is to save some time before bed to go through your checklist, pack up everything you need to bring to school, and set out the clothes you want to wear the next day.

Checklists and to-do lists are great tools to keep track of everything. For instance, you can have a morning checklist to help you get ready for school faster or a bedtime checklist to help you get ready for bed on time. Likewise, a backpack checklist is perfect to help you remember everything you need to bring to school.

Fill in the blanks with your morning, bedtime, and backpack checklist. You can decide what to put on your list and consult with a trusted adult if you are stuck.

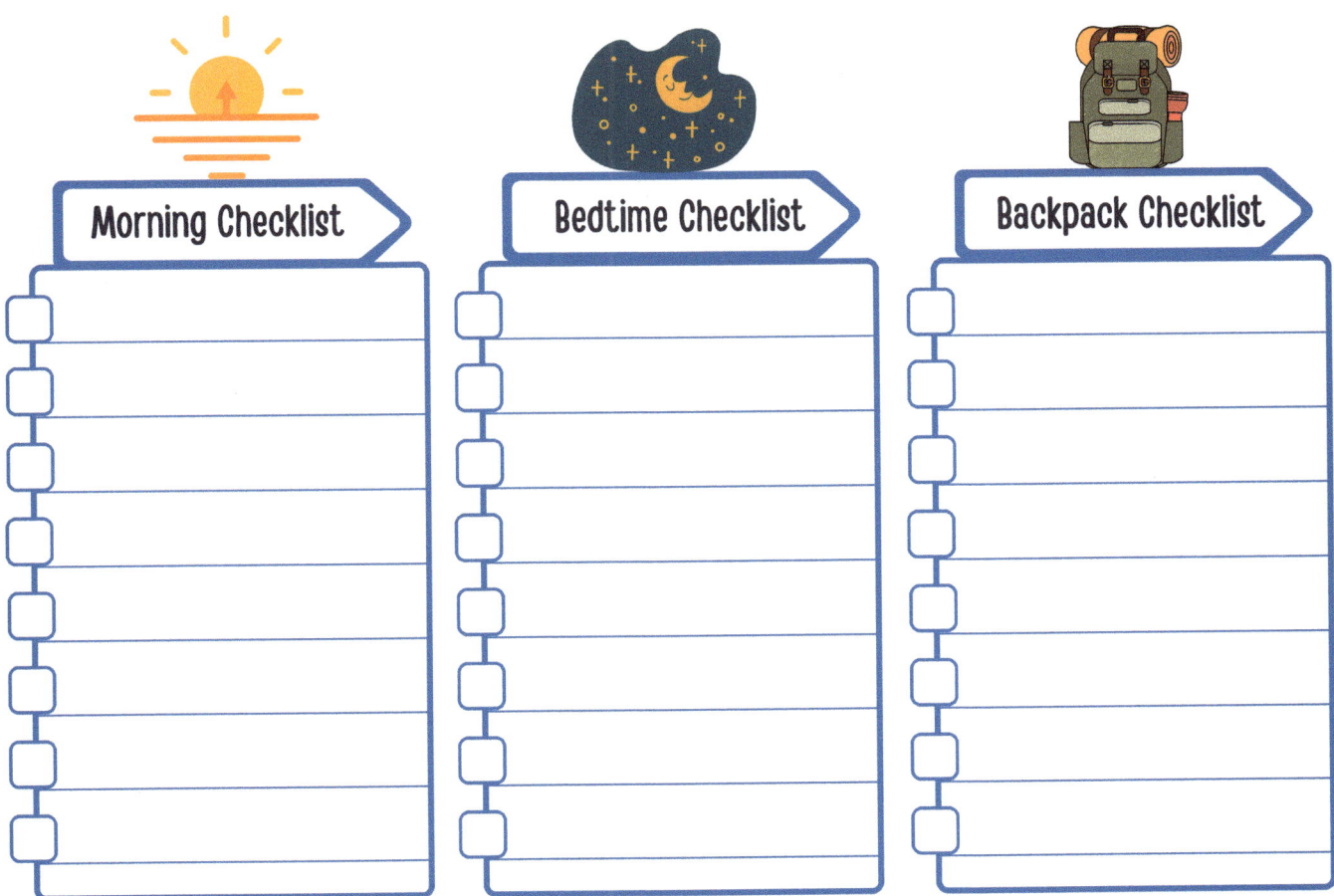

Morning Checklist

Bedtime Checklist

Backpack Checklist

Planning also involves making schedules. For example, check out Pepper's schedule for his art project below. Like Pepper, you can make a schedule to list every step you need to accomplish a task.

Pepper's Art Project Checklist

- ✅ Read the directions and ask for help if needed
- ☐ Get my pencil, crayon, glitter, glue, scissors, and paper
- ☐ Draw an outline
- ☐ Add color, add glitter, and cut out artwork
- ☐ Check work for last-minute edits
- ☐ Place the artwork inside my folder and school backpack

My _____ Checklist

- ☐ _____
- ☐ _____
- ☐ _____
- ☐ _____
- ☐ _____
- ☐ _____

Marking My Calendars

Have you ever been overwhelmed by too many events or tasks happening all at once? Writing down your activities on a calendar or an e-calendar can help you see everything and track what you must do. For example, you can put down school events, deadlines, extracurricular activities, or appointments on your monthly calendar. It is often easier to see a physical plan than keep everything in your head. Although sometimes people can get by without a checklist, having one can help prevent forgetting important details—especially if there are many tasks.

If you feel like your calendar needs to be more organized, you can use color codes or multiple calendars to help. For example, you can use a red-colored marker for test dates and another color for fun activities. Once you do this, it will become much easier to mentally prepare for a particular task or look forward to happy times! If you find colors less useful, you can use multiple calendars—one for school and another for personal events. It will take some time to find what works for you, but you will see wonderful results from planning ahead once you start!

Here is a two-week calendar example:

Month: October				Year: 2023		
Sunday	**Monday**	**Tuesday**	**Wednesday**	**Thursday**	**Friday**	**Saturday**
1 Bring Book to School Tomorrow	2	3	4	5 Math Test	6	7 Dentist Appointment
8	9	10 Soccer Practice	11	12	13 Book Report Due	14 Ashley's Birthday Party

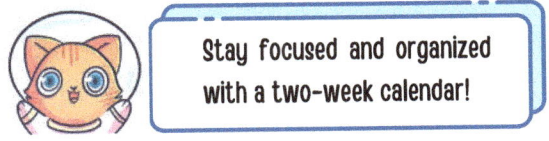

Stay focused and organized with a two-week calendar!

Sometimes, plans may change, things do not go as planned, or maybe some important events come up on short notice. If any changes occur, make sure to fix your calendar. It is helpful to select a time, like Saturday mornings, to review and update your weekly calendar. Doing this will help you become more effective!

Pro Tip: E-calendars like Google Calendar may be easier to use because you can adjust by dragging an event to a different time slot and easily insert new tasks.

Fill in the empty calendar below by placing important events under each day. You can also draw your own calendar, use an e-calendar like Google Calendar, or buy a physical calendar.

My Two-Week Calendar:

Month:

Year:

Sunday	Monday	Tuesday	Wednesday	Thursday	Friday	Saturday
☐	☐	☐	☐	☐	☐	☐
☐	☐	☐	☐	☐	☐	☐

You are making great progress! You are on your way to becoming a pro planner. Do not give up, and keep pushing yourself to learn new skills.

Making Plans

President Benjamin Franklin once said: "failing to plan is planning to fail." Learning how to plan is crucial for success. To practice, you can help plan for activities on the weekend like a slumber party or an outdoor activity. Try this planning exercise. Imagine you are planning a one-day trip to somewhere far away. Answer the following questions:

Where will you go?

_____

Who will go with you?

_____

When will you go?

_____

How will you get there?

_____

What materials will you need to bring?

_____

When will you have to wake up?

_____

When will you need to leave home?

_____

When will you have to get home?

_____

How will you get home?

_____

Plan the activities from morning to evening by making a schedule. Write each activity below and the time you will start and finish each step.

For example:

⏰	Morning (a.m.)	⏰	Afternoon (p.m.)	⏰	Evening (p.m.)
7:00-8:00	Wake up and get ready	12:00-2:00	Go on a hike	6:00-7:00	Drive home
8:00-9:00	Drive to the beach	2:00-4:00	Go surfing	7:00	Arrive home
9:00-11:00	Play volleyball	4:00-5:00	Build sandcastles		
11:00-12:00	Eat lunch	5:00-6:00	Eat dinner		

Plan your day:

⏰	Morning (a.m.)	⏰	Afternoon (p.m.)	⏰	Evening (p.m.)

Can you think of anything else you need to add to your plan?

_____

_____

_____

_____

Will you be able to do everything in one day? If not, then it is time to adjust your plan so that you can get back home on time!

_____

_____

_____

_____

Bora's Pro Tip: As Harry Truman once said, "Imperfect action is better than perfect inaction." Your work does not need to be perfect! You just need to keep working on your skills because working on them is better than not working on them at all.

Help Pepper Plan

"Help! I need to throw a surprise birthday party for my friend, but I don't know how to plan it! The party is supposed to take place this weekend, but there's so much to do, and I don't know where to start. Can you help me? This is the last challenge for you on this planet. I will give you my crystal if you can help me plan!"

Make a checklist for Pepper so he knows which steps he needs to take to plan a fun birthday party. You can suggest things like picking the time, choosing a place, or buying decorations—anything you can think of. Let your imagination run wild and help Pepper plan the best birthday party ever!

Birthday Party Checklist

☐ _____

☐ _____

☐ _____

☐ _____

☐ _____

☐ _____

Pepper, the Dog:

"Oh! I am so excited! My friend is going to love the surprise party. Thank you for helping. Here is the crystal you need! Oh—and did you decide if I can be your best friend? Never mind, I'll stop bothering you."

You just received another crystal. You now have four and need four more to go!

Congratulations on reaching the halfway point! You are doing so well. There are only four more crystals to get until you can save humanity from the evil aliens. Keep your eye on the prize, and keep pushing!

When there are multiple tasks to complete, you need to decide which task needs to be done before others—that is called prioritizing. Head to the next planet to learn more about it!

Break Time: Spend 10 minutes teaching someone what you just learned. Sharing what you learned will help you understand better!

Next Stop

Planet Priority

Planet Goals

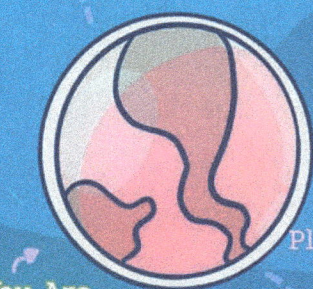
Planet Planner

You Are Here

Planet Knowledge

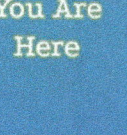

Planet Skills

Planet Reflection

Planet Executive

Planet Earth

Chapter 5
Planet Priority

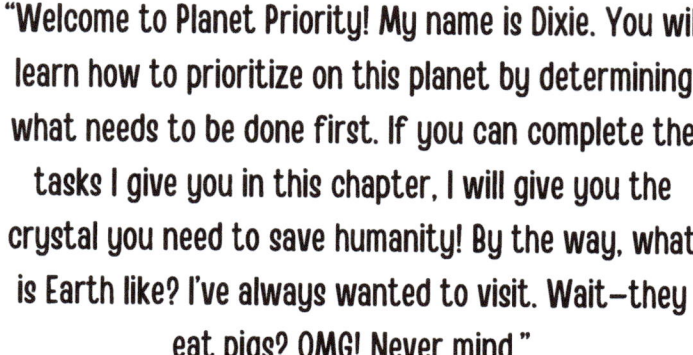

"Welcome to Planet Priority! My name is Dixie. You will learn how to prioritize on this planet by determining what needs to be done first. If you can complete the tasks I give you in this chapter, I will give you the crystal you need to save humanity! By the way, what is Earth like? I've always wanted to visit. Wait—they eat pigs? OMG! Never mind."

Prioritizing Skills Deep Dive

Have you ever felt overwhelmed by a long list of tasks and did not know where to start? Have you ever realized that you should have done something else first before starting a task? These things can happen if you do not know how to prioritize—knowing how to prioritize means determining which tasks require your attention first.

Here is an example:

Dixie has a lot of hobbies. She loves to swim and play soccer. She also loves hanging out with friends and volunteering in her community. After participating in all these hobbies, she usually ends up with very little time and energy to do her homework; and she is getting a poor grade at school because of that. If she wants to improve her grade, she must complete her homework first before enjoying her hobbies. Since homework has due dates and demands more focus, that should be done first; and since hanging out with friends does not require too much energy, that should be done later.

The aliens are still abducting humans. Our only hope is the brave hero opening Stargate!

News Tip
In order to be great at prioritizing, ask yourself, "which task needs to be done before the others?"

Color Me

Why Prioritize?

Everybody needs to prioritize because the order is important. You can usually get more things done if you complete them in the right order. Even the most capable superheroes need to prioritize when they are on a mission. Take the superhero Flash, for instance—he can run super-fast, but he still needs to prioritize because he cannot get to all places at once. So, if he has multiple people he needs to save, he must decide which person he needs to get to first and which person he can get to later—that is prioritizing.

Prioritizing involves arranging tasks by ordering them according to their level of importance and thinking about which ones you should do first. Start with the most important task first, then move on to the less important tasks afterward. After practicing how to prioritize, you will feel more guided when you have lots of tasks to do. You will be able to do the most important task first and resist doing the first thing that comes to mind—which is usually not the best thing to do. When you have many tasks to complete, stay calm, take a second to plan, and determine which task you need to do first.

Remember your three strengths and use them to keep pushing forward!

What Is More Urgent?

To determine which task should be done first, you must think about what will happen if you fail to complete each option. Typically, more bad things will happen if you do not do the most important task first. For example, if somebody is at the door, but something is burning, which one needs your attention first? That is right—you probably want to put out the fire before you answer the door, or else the house might catch on fire. The person can wait, but the fire cannot.

In the exercise below, read the task, then check which step should be done before the other:

1. I have math homework due tomorrow and an art project due in one month. What should I do first?
- [ ] Art project
- [ ] Math homework

2. My friend invited me to the movies, but I have a big test tomorrow. What should I do first?
- [ ] Go to the movies
- [ ] Study for my big test

3. I I have to catch a bus at 6 a.m. tomorrow, but my new video game just arrived. What should I do first?
- [ ] Sleep early
- [ ] Play my game past bedtime

4. My new Pokemon book just arrived, but I am having trouble with my homework that is due tomorrow. What should I do first?
- [ ] Ask for help with my homework
- [ ] Read the Pokemon book

5. I am running late for school, but my favorite TV show has a new episode. What should I do first?

☐ Watch TV
☐ Get ready for school

6. I want to go to the swimming pool, but my dog just ran away. What should I do first?

☐ Go swimming
☐ Find my dog

7. It is time for my violin lesson, but my friend wants to discuss her birthday party with me over the phone. What should I do first?

☐ Talk to my friend about her party
☐ Go to my violin lesson

8. My mom asked me to watch the pasta on the stove, and it's starting to burn, but I am about to beat the boss on my video game. What should I do first?

☐ Finish playing the game
☐ Stop the pasta from burning

What Comes First?

Do you enjoy eating hamburgers? You might have eaten some at a restaurant or made them at home. Typically, you need to prepare the ingredients before cooking your hamburgers. You need to make sure you have your buns, vegetables, spread, and raw burger patties readied. When you have everything ready, you can start cooking the hamburger patties. You do not want to cook the patties first because it takes time to prepare the rest of the ingredients, and your hamburger will get cold!

The burger is a great example of prioritizing. When we decide to prepare the ingredients before cooking, we look ahead to see what needs to be done first for the process to go smoothly. The same goes for any activity. Think ahead and prioritize each step carefully before you start a task. You do not want to start an assignment only to find out you left something at school—just like you do not want to start cooking a burger only to find out you are missing the buns!

What Are My Big Rocks?

Prioritizing can be very hard if you have too many tasks. In fact, many adults struggle with this, too. At first, everything may seem equally important, but as you get more familiar with prioritizing, you will see that a few things are typically more important than others.

You may wonder: how do I decide what is more important? Good question! A person's priorities should be based on their goals and dreams. For example, if you want to become an Olympic swimmer, you should prioritize swimming. If you want to be a writer, you need to value writing and reading over other tasks.

Optional exercise:

You will need:
- 1 small jar
- big rocks
- pebbles
- sand

1. Grab a glass jar like a mason jar, some big rocks, some pebbles, and sand. Try to fit all your sand in the jar first, insert the pebbles second, and the big rocks last. Do they all fit into the jar? You might notice that there is not enough room for your big rocks after fitting in your sand and pebbles.
2. Empty the jar and insert the big rocks first, then the pebbles second, and the sand last. Did you notice that everything now fits in the jar?

Big rocks (must do today)

Pebbles (should do today)

Sand (would like to do today)

Pro Tip: The big rocks are your priorities. They take up the most space and should always go in first. The pebbles and sand can always fit into the cracks later, but not the other way around. If you choose to fit the pebbles or sand first, then you will run out of space (your time) for the big rocks (your priorities)!

Now, we will explore a little bit more on how to determine priorities. First, list out all the tasks you want to do today. For example:

1. Complete my homework for tomorrow's classes.
2. Play Roblox.
3. Start on a project that is due in one month.
4. Get my friend a birthday gift for his birthday in a few days.
5. Cook a meal for my family.

Second, give each activity one of these labels: **"Must do today,"** **"Should do today,"** or **"Would like to do today."** Doing this will help you see which task needs to be done right now and which task can be done later.

Activities	Labels
1.	
2.	
3.	
4.	
5.	

Bora's Pro Tip: Sometimes, you need to rely on others for support and guidance. If you feel lost and unsure, talk to your guardian or trusted friends. Sometimes, just talking to people can help you come up with solutions!

Long-Term Projects

Getting started on big projects or essays can be stressful. You may feel unsure where to start because it seems like a lot of work. Planning and prioritizing will help you see a clear path to success. Think of it as a puzzle. You need to know how the finished puzzle looks before you start!

It is very simple to plan and prioritize for a long-term project. Here are the four steps:

1. List out all the tasks you need to do to complete the project.
2. Note the due date on your calendar and see how many days you have to work with.
3. Assign tasks for each day leading up to the due date—starting with the most important tasks first.
4. Check with your guardian weekly to make sure you are making steady progress, and adjust your schedule if things change.

Try this exercise below. Your teacher assigned you a book report due in one month. Read the following tasks below, then number the tasks in order starting with number one being your top priority.

☐ Check the due date and mark it on your calendar.

☐ Pick out a book you want to write about.

☐ Write your first draft.

☐ Submit the project.

☐ Double-check your final draft with a trusted adult.

☐ Make final changes to your report.

☐ Plan your report with an outline.

☐ Finish reading the book.

☐ Proofread and edit your first draft.

Help Dixie Prioritize

"Help! I ruined my boss's house, and now he is demanding that I build a new one for him in only seven days or else he will send me to another planet! I am panicking because I don't have time! I don't even know where to start! Can you help me organize my thoughts and tell me where I should begin? I will give you the crystal you need if you help me."

Here is a list of things that Dixie can think of while she is worried. She needs a calm mind to help her sort through the tasks and put them in the correct order. Can you help her? Remember, with each line, ask yourself: will this task help Dixie accomplish her goal?

Identify five necessary tasks, cross out the unimportant ones and rank the five tasks in order of importance, starting with number one, the top priority.

- ☐ Complain to her friends about how her boss is unreasonable.

- ☐ Figure out what materials are needed for the house.

- ☐ Draw a blueprint for the house.

- ☐ Do something fun for a day and forget about it.

- ☐ Gather the materials you need to build the house.

- ☐ Gather villagers to help build the house.

- ☐ Use the calendar and plan what needs to be done each day.

- ☐ Start building the house by yourself and hope for the best.

Dixie, the Pig:

"Thank you so much! I can't believe I will build it on time. I thought I would be gone for sure! Oh right, here's your crystal. Good luck on your journey!"

You just received another crystal. You now have five and only need three more to save Planet Earth! Way to go!

If you put together all the planning and prioritizing skills from the previous chapters, you will have everything you need to achieve long-term goals and succeed in life. Now, fly to the next planet to learn more about goals.

Break Time: Spend 10 minutes teaching someone what you just learned. Sharing what you learned will help you understand better!

Planet Priority

You Are
Here

Next
Stop

Planet Goals

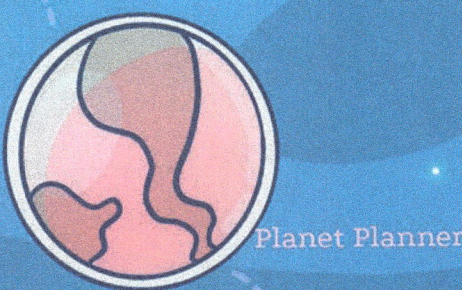
Planet Planner

Planet Knowledge

Planet Skills

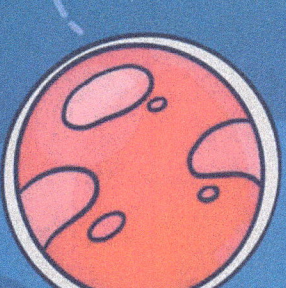
Planet Reflection

Planet Executive

Planet Earth

Chapter 6
Planet Goals

> "Welcome to Planet Goals! My name is Starla. You will learn about goals and how to make them on this planet. I will reward you with this shiny crystal if you can finish my requests! I'm not really sure what this is for, but you seem to like it... And just because I'm a robot does not mean I don't have feelings! Oh wait, you weren't thinking that. Okay, this is awkward—bye!"

Setting Goals

You will learn about setting goals in this chapter. Goals are the things we want to achieve within a specific timeframe. There are short-term and long-term goals: a short-term goal is a target you can reach within days or weeks, and a long-term goal is something you can achieve in months or years. For example, if you want to learn how to bake a pie, that can probably be done within days or weeks—hence it is a short-term goal. On the other hand, if you have a big dream of becoming a champion baker, that would be a long-term goal because it may require years of experience and practice.

How to Achieve Long-Term Goals

Long-term goals can be a lot to handle all at once, but breaking them up into short-term goals is an effective way to manage them. For instance, before you can become a champion baker, you might want to accomplish the following short-term goals: learn how to bake a pie, learn how to bake a cake, get a job at a bakery, or work for a champion baker.

Achieving short-term goals can help you gain momentum and remain excited about your long-term goals. Without them, you may not feel like you are progressing much since long-term goals can seem really far away. Instead, if you set deadlines to achieve short-term goals one by one, you will know that you are making steady progress, and you will gain the confidence to keep going. Then, if you follow your plan, your dream will soon become a reality.

Tip Corner:

- Stay motivated by always remembering your WHY.
- Your WHY is the reason you want to achieve the goal.
- Having a strong WHY will help you overcome difficult times.
- You can make posters of your WHY and put them all over your room.
- For example, Nathan wants to play pro basketball, so he has Lebron James posters everywhere!
- Lila wants to perform at Coachella one day, so she has Coachella pictures as her desktop image!

Color Me

Story Time

For Starla, the Robot, her long-term goal is to build a spaceship so she can find a true friend in this lonely galaxy. However, building a spaceship seems very hard without creating a roadmap. So, she needs to break her long-term goal into short-term goals to make it easier. She can do this by first getting a blueprint for the spaceship and gathering all the machine parts. She would then have to build the engine, the pilot seat, the wings, and the rest of the parts before piecing them together. Whenever she feels unmotivated, she remembers her WHY to keep pushing her forward. She drew a painting of her playing with her future best friend and placed it next to her bed. Remember earlier when we said it is crucial to know why you want to achieve a goal? This painting helps Starla remember every day that she is building a spaceship to find her one true friend.

You are doing a great job so far! Feel free to take short breaks if you are exhausted. Just remember to return to finish the activities as soon as you are recharged. You will accomplish your goals as long as you keep making progress. You only fail if you give up!

The Present and the Future

Do you have trouble deciding what a goal is? A goal is not like doing homework, brushing your teeth, or getting ready for bed—those are tasks you need to do every day. Instead, a goal is like winning a competition, joining the basketball team, getting an A in school, or performing in public. Those are goals because you need to create plans for them and work hard to achieve them.

Here is a helpful activity to see what can be identified as a goal:

First, write down a list of all the things you want to have, do, or become. Feel free to write down anything that comes to mind.

Things I Want

Next, separate the items on the list into two columns. In the "Present" column, assign items you can achieve over a day or two. Items like cleaning your room, getting new clothes, or getting a haircut belong here. In the "Future" column, assign items that typically take much longer to achieve. Items like becoming a millionaire, competing in the Olympics, or saving up for a car will go here.

Present

Future

Would you believe me if I told you that the things you wrote down in the "Present" column are not goals but tasks? That is because you can typically achieve them without too much planning. The items you wrote in your "Future" column will be your goals because goals are not something you can obtain quickly.

What Is My Goal?

Take a look at your "Future" list from the previous activity, and pick a goal you want to achieve the most. It can be something you want to improve on or someone you want to become when you are older. For example, you may want to be the captain of the soccer team or become a movie star. Write your goal inside the star—make sure you can clearly define the goal.

After choosing a goal, write down your WHY—why do you want to do it? It is important to know what achieving the goal can help you do. Remember why you are working towards your goal, as that will help you keep going even when things get rough.

What is my goal?

What is my WHY?

_____

_____

My Game Plan

By this time, you should have chosen a goal and thought about why you want to achieve it. This is a long-term goal because it will take time and effort.

Just like how athletes need game plans to help win games, you need a plan to help you achieve your goal. Now, we will guide you to break up your long-term goal into some short-term goals.

First, list out what you need to do to achieve your goal. Suppose your goal is to become a singer; you might need to take singing lessons, practice singing every day, or join the school choir. Feel free to ask your friends and family for ideas if you are unsure.

My Goal To-Do List

1. _____
2. _____
3. _____
4. _____
5. _____
6. _____
7. _____
8. _____
9. _____
10. _____

After listing everything out, determine which short-term goals are most important, less important, and least important. By now, you should start to see which one you will need to achieve first. You should always track your progress by revisiting this list and make sure you are always working on the most important goals. The most important short-term goals will be more difficult, but you should do them first. Once you achieve most of your short-term goals, you should be pretty close to achieving your long-term goal!

Most Important

Less Important

Least Important

Marking My Calendar

In Chapter 4, we learned how to use a two-week calendar. For this exercise, use a monthly calendar that you can assign a due date for the short-term goals on your game plan. Please mark the calendar below or use your own calendar.

Month:		Year:	

Sunday	Monday	Tuesday	Wednesday	Thursday	Friday	Saturday
☐	☐	☐	☐	☐	☐	☐
☐	☐	☐	☐	☐	☐	☐
☐	☐	☐	☐	☐	☐	☐
☐	☐	☐	☐	☐	☐	☐
☐	☐	☐	☐	☐	☐	☐

Now that you have assigned dates for these short-term goals, continue to keep track of your progress by checking them off your calendar as you fulfill them. This will help you visualize your progress and keep you on track to reach your ultimate goal. You will learn how to do this in the next activity!

Tracking My Progress

You might feel lost as you progress through your game plan and calendar. Below are some questions you can ask yourself after a couple of weeks if you feel unsure. Answer the questions below, and make changes to your game plan if needed:

1 Am I progressing every day, even if just a little bit?

_____

_____

2 What is the most important thing I must do next?

_____

_____

3 Is there anything I do not need to do?

_____

_____

4 If I am stuck, what is the challenge I am facing? Can anyone help me with it?

_____

_____

Bora's Pro Tip: Many things take more time and do not happen as planned. It is normal to experience setbacks or challenges along the way. If changes occur, modify your plan and keep checking off the list daily.

Help Starla With Her Goal

"Help! I don't know if these are considered goals or tasks. Can you help me categorize them? This is the last challenge on this planet. I'll give you this extremely rare crystal if you help me."

Is this a goal?

Circle the items that can be goals:

Take a nap.

Change out my batteries.

Build a robot dog from scratch.

Travel around the galaxy.

Read the entire book collection on astrology.

Eat some bolts and screws for lunch.

Water my plants.

Learn a new language.

Starla, the Robot:

"Thanks for helping! I always felt bored because I didn't have any goals, but now I can finally live my life with a purpose and never be bored again! Oh, and here is the crystal you were looking for."

You just received another crystal. You now have six and need two more to go!

Now you know how to plan, prioritize, and achieve long-term goals. Head to the next planet now. We will make sure you understand everything you have learned.

Break Time: Spend 10 minutes teaching someone what you just learned. Sharing what you learned will help you understand better!

Planet Priority

You Are Here

Planet Goals

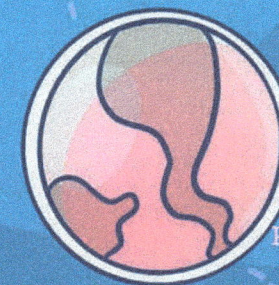

Planet Planner

Next Stop

Planet Knowledge

Planet Skills

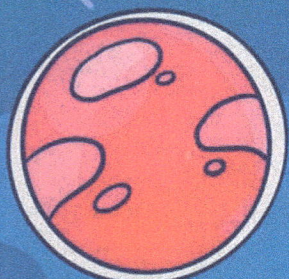

Planet Reflection

Planet Executive

Planet Earth

Chapter 7

Planet Knowledge

"Welcome to Planet Knowledge. My name is Doodle! Your knowledge will be tested on this planet. If you complete the following challenges, you will be rewarded with one of the last crystals you are looking for! Did I mention my name is Doodle? Doodle, the Bird. I will be the fastest bird on this planet one day. You just wait and see!"

Testing My Knowledge

Before we get started, here is a fun fact:

Did you know that certain animals can also plan ahead? Besides humans and apes, ravens are the only other animals with superb planning abilities. When scientists gave different tools to swap for food, ravens ALWAYS chose the right tools; and they even showed the ability to wait longer for bigger rewards. Be patient and plan ahead like ravens!

What Would You Do?

This exercise will test your knowledge by asking "what would you do?" questions in different settings. Help these people by writing down what you would do in their positions. Try your best and ask for help if you get stuck.

 **1**

Kayla always turned in her homework on time, but when she received a long-term project from her teacher, she started having trouble. She did not know where to start and which task to start first. She knows she can ask for help, but she wants to try it out on her own first.

What would you do? Remember, you can get the answer to this question on Planet Planner in Chapter 4.

_____

_____

_____

_____

2

Sam has been looking for his favorite pants for over a week. He knows that the pants are somewhere in his room, but the thought of cleaning up his room makes him feel overwhelmed. He keeps telling himself that he will do it, but he is unsure where to begin and keeps delaying the task.

What would you do? Remember, you can get the answer on Planet Planner in Chapter 4.

_____

_____

_____

_____

3 Jimmy is a social butterfly. He loves talking to his friends online all day, but he often forgets to do his homework, so now he has a bad grade in his class. He wants to improve his grades, but he is unsure how.

What would you do? Remember, you can get the answer on Planet Priority in Chapter 5.

_____

_____

_____

_____

4 Monae started making singing videos because she wanted to become famous, just like her idol Harry Styles. After months of making videos, she has not gained any followers. She sometimes feels discouraged and forgets why she should even bother.

What would you do? Remember, you can get the answer on Planet Goals in Chapter 6.

_____

_____

_____

_____

Bora's Pro Tip: Many little actions over time create big changes. Keep checking off your short-term goals, and you will do wonders!

Doodle's Game Plan

"Help! I want to be the fastest bird on this planet because I want to save other birds when they need help, but I don't know how to achieve that goal. I need help planning and prioritizing each step to make my goal a reality! Can you help me? I will give you the crystal you're searching for if you help me."

Help Doodle create his game plan. Take everything you learned from the previous chapters and help him make a checklist, arrange the steps in order of importance, and determine his WHY. Feel free to revisit the previous chapters to help you.

○ ....

○ ....

○ ....

○ ....

○ ....

○ ....

○ ....

○ ....

WHY?

....

Doodle, the Bird:

"Oooh! Thank you so much for making a game plan for my goal. I will become the fastest bird on this planet with this plan! Yippy! Here is the crystal you need!"

You just received another crystal. You now have seven and need just one more to save Planet Earth!

Great job learning everything about planning, prioritizing, and setting goals. With learning, it is always great to do some self-reflection. Fly to the next planet now to grab the last crystal and complete your journey!

Break Time: Spend 10 minutes teaching someone what you just learned. Sharing what you learned will help you understand better!

Planet Priority

Planet Goals

Planet Planner

You Are
Here

Planet Knowledge

Planet Skills

Next
Stop

Planet Reflection

Planet Executive

Planet Earth

Chapter 8

Planet Reflection

> "Yay—you have made it to Planet Reflection! You are kind of famous around here. Everyone is talking about how well you are doing and how you will save Planet Earth. I can't believe you decided to take on the aliens yourself! My name is Zuri. You will answer self-reflection questions on this planet. You can get the last crystal from me to complete your mission."

Self-Reflection

Great job for making it to the final planet! In this chapter, we will be reflecting on how to use the lessons learned in this workbook for future challenges.

As you grow up and take on more challenges, remember these **six key takeaways:**

1 You can succeed if you make consistent progress daily—even baby steps count!

2 Plan out your tasks before you start anything.

3 Break down difficult tasks or goals into easier steps and form a game plan.

4 Prioritize and always do the most important things on the list first.

5 Remember why you want to achieve your goals and install reminders in your personal space.

6 Be courageous and ask for help when you are uncertain what to do next.

Extra Pro Tips:

⭐ Remember the three strengths you listed for yourself at the beginning of this book? Find ways to use these strengths more when facing new challenges!

⭐ It is normal to revise your timelines and adjust your schedule as you go. Things do not always go according to plan in life, but a good planner can adjust and get back in control quickly!

⭐ Use positive thoughts to motivate yourself. Stand in front of a mirror and say positive things to boost your confidence. Try saying things like: I am unique; I am brave; I am smart; I won't give up; I am loved; or, I am going to overcome this challenge because I know how to plan and prioritize.

⭐ Try not to think about mistakes or bad results for too long. Everybody makes mistakes, but true champions learn from them fast and move on quickly. Stay confident in your abilities and use your mistakes to help you grow.

⭐ Share what you learned here with your friends and family. Maybe your classmates have different tips that can help you improve, or maybe your friends need help with their planning skills. Talking to people will help you understand the material better.

⭐ Finally, you can always revisit this workbook to refresh your memory. Although you will face many different challenges in the future, the techniques in this book are useful for even very old adults!

Conquering New Challenges

Part of growing is learning new skills and taking on new challenges. Whenever you have an opportunity to learn new skills, always remain open to learning and applying them because they can help you achieve your goals. After reaching your goals, ask yourself: what new challenges can I conquer next?

Answer the following questions below:

1. What are some new goals you would like to work on in the future?
- You can revisit some goals you wanted to reach in the past.
- You can build on the goals you have already reached and make them more challenging. For example, if you joined the choir last year, you might want to become the choir leader this year.
- If nothing comes to mind, try finishing these sentences: **"I want to be...", "I want to do...", and "I want to have...".**

_____

_____

_____

_____

_____

2. Write down your **WHY**. Why do you want to accomplish these goals?

_____

_____

_____

_____

You can write down your new goals on a sheet of paper and post them somewhere visible to remember them every day.

Final Thoughts

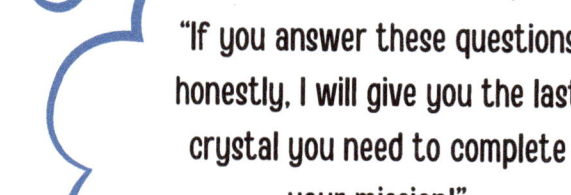

"If you answer these questions honestly, I will give you the last crystal you need to complete your mission!"

Zuri would like to know your final thoughts. Answer the following questions below:

 How do you think you did, and why?

_____

_____

 Which activity was the most helpful to you, and why?

_____

_____

 Which skill was the most helpful to you, and why?

_____

_____

 Which skill will you need to work on more, and why?

_____

_____

 Can you think of anyone who might benefit from these new skills you just learned in this workbook? Who are they, and why?

_____

_____

Zuri, the Monkey:

"Oh wow, seems like you've got a lot of good things coming your way! Don't forget about me when you become a hero! And make sure to share your knowledge with the friends you thought of during the last activity. Ta-dah—here is the last crystal you need. We shall be hearing songs about your heroic act across the galaxy soon!"

You just received your last crystal. You now have all eight crystals to save Planet Earth!

Fly back to Planet Earth to activate Stargate and send the aliens back to where they belong!

Break Time: Spend 10 minutes teaching someone what you just learned. Sharing what you learned will help you understand better!

Planet Priority

Planet Goals

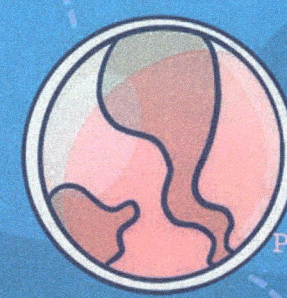
Planet Planner

Planet Knowledge

Planet Skills

You Are
Here

Planet Reflection

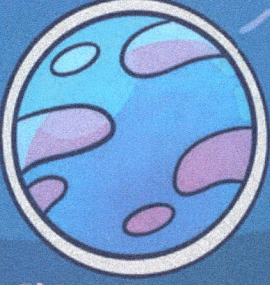
Planet Executive

Next
Stop

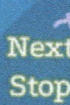

Planet Earth

"You did it! You collected all eight crystals and successfully sent the evil aliens back to their planet. The humans salute you and present you with a medal of honor!"

Goodbye, Aliens!

You opened Stargate!

You Are a Champion!

End this journey in style! In the box below, draw yourself as a hero for collecting all eight crystals and saving Planet Earth from the aliens. Now that you have gained new skills, write down two new strengths of yours and draw items around your character to represent them— add these to your list of superpowers that you can rely on to overcome any challenge!

Two New Strengths:

 1 _____

2 _____

I am very proud of you for completing each activity and finding all the crystals. Please collect your reward from your trusted adult—the one you agreed to at the beginning of this journey. You have done such a great job learning new skills. The skills you have acquired from this book are also a massive reward. They can be applied to many other areas in your life and help you accomplish ANYTHING!

If you liked this adventure, be sure to check out our other workbooks. More adventures are waiting to be explored in our other Executive Functioning Workbooks. Collect all of the executive functioning skills to become the Ultimate Achiever. See you on the next mission!

Answers

Challenge #2: All About Executive Functioning Skills

1. True: If you improve your executive functioning skills, you can overcome difficult challenges.
2. False: Adults use executive functioning skills too.
3. False: Executive functioning skills are used to do just about anything.
4. True: You need executive functioning skills to play sports.
5. True: You use executive functioning skills to plan trips.
6. False: You need executive functioning skills to do everyday tasks.
7. True: You can learn new executive functioning skills.
8. True: Practicing your executive functioning skills will help you improve them like any other skill.
9. False: Everyone uses executive functioning skills.
10. True: You use executive functioning skills to learn, read, and do homework.

Challenge #5: Fill in the Blank

1. Planning
2. Prioritizing
3. calendar
4. challenging
5. time

Challenge #22: What Would You Do?

1. Kayla can break up her project into smaller steps, make a checklist on her calendar, and assign her own deadlines for each step until the project's due date. She can update her progress regularly by crossing off any completed steps or rearranging her calendar if plans change.
2. Sam can break up the tasks into smaller steps and label each step from 1-10—1 being the easiest and 10 being the hardest. If any of the steps are too difficult, he can break them down into smaller, level 3 steps.
3. Jimmy can list out all the things he wants to do and arrange them according to the level of importance. He can complete his homework assignments first before talking to his friends.
4. Monae can remember her WHY, which is to become famous like her idol Harry Styles. She can put reminders all over her room to help her remember this: posters, screenshots, or pictures are all good choices!

Leave a Review

Reviews are essential to our livelihood as a small independent publisher. Please leave a review for our product so we can continue to serve more families with similar needs. If you have any comments or suggestions, please reach out to our website and send us a message. Thank you so much for helping our small business survive!

Sign Up Below

Sign up by visiting the website below to get updates on our future book releases! The subsequent workbooks will cover topics like task initiation, time management, emotional control, and more. Stay tuned, and don't miss out!

Visit www.edchievellc.com/publishing

About the Author

Roy D. Pan, Ph.D., is a seasoned educator who has worked with over 550 students in Asia and North America. He owns Edchieve, LLC—an education consulting company that helps students with executive functioning skills, life skills, and self-improvement. He promotes independent learning and focuses on the inside-out approach to motivate his students. His lessons are derived from the teachings of his father, a former Professor of Pharmacology at NYMU, Taipei, and his UCLA Ph.D. mentor, Professor Michael Jung, inventor of the billion-dollar drug Xtandi.

Dr. Pan enjoys many side hobbies such as cooking, watching sports, playing basketball, swimming, and reading books, but his main hobby is teaching, and he loves to see his students succeed. He wrote this book because he has personally seen many families troubled by executive functioning challenges. He hopes this book will provide a wonderful learning experience for many families and that children can use these lessons to enjoy tackling challenges and achieving personal goals.

www.ingramcontent.com/pod-product-compliance
Lightning Source LLC
Chambersburg PA
CBHW041539120626
46551CB00019B/2764